CONTENTS

POLICE LINE DO NOT CROSS

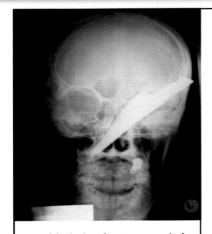

Cause of death: sharp force trauma – a knife blow to the head. Manner of death: murder!

Death has five faces. It can be natural: an aging heart stops ticking or lungs give in to cancer. It can be an accident: a car crash or a bad fall. It can be a suicide: someone takes his or her own life. Sometimes, the manner of death is a mystery: the cause is 'undetermined'. This book is about the fifth face of death: murder – when one person kills another.

A smoking gun

Murder is the gravest crime there is, and it takes a team of experts to solve every case: crime scene investigators who collect evidence at the crime scene; profilers who explore the criminal mind; and crime lab technicians who test blood, bullets, and other evidence.

All these experts are looking for a 'smoking gun' – the big clue that cracks a murder case. But remember, sometimes 'the smoking gun' isn't actually a gun at all. It might not even be a weapon. Sometimes, 'the smoking gun' is a corpse! The dead body itself holds clues to solving its own murder.

Take the case of American serial killer Ted Bundy. In the 1970s, this outwardly charming man was the main suspect in at least thirty-six murders.

His killing spree stretched from Washington State to Florida, with a bloody trail across several other states in between. Bundy left behind little evidence – no fingerprints, no weapons, and, in some cases, no body. Several victims simply went missing, never to be seen again.

Then, in 1978, a 'smoking gun' clue was found on a body: the skin had a bite mark. Ted Bundy's slightly crooked teeth matched the bite mark perfectly. This physical evidence linked him directly to the crime. Bundy was convicted of murder and later confessed to many more killings, all of young women and girls. In 1989, he was executed in Florida in the electric chair.

Dr. Lowell J. Levine, forensic odontologist (far right), testifies in court that the bite marks (circled in red, right) found on the murder victim show characteristics of Ted Bundy's teeth (center).

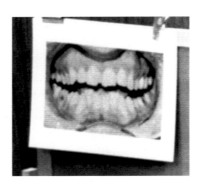

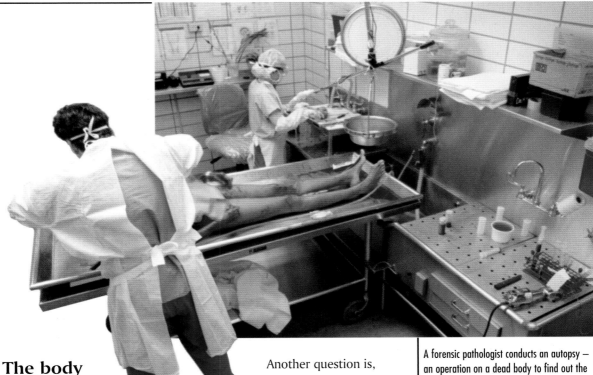

A forensic pathologist conducts an autopsy – an operation on a dead body to find out the manner and cause of death.

The body as evidence

As evidence, a corpse must be searched, bit by bit, inside and out – in just the same way as a crime scene. The body search is called an autopsy, which is an operation usually done by a forensic pathologist. They are both a doctor and a crime scientist. He or she knows how to examine and interpret injuries as evidence – to explain what they prove, or don't prove, about the person's death.

Every science investigation is driven by questions. In a murder case, the pathologist doesn't ask, "Who did it?" – that's for detectives to figure out. They ask: "What did it? What was the cause of death?

Another question is, "What was the manner of death?" Manner and cause aren't the same thing. Manner is one of those 'five faces' – natural, accident, suicide, undetermined or murder. If a body has no name, the pathologist also asks, "Who are you?"

The quest for answers begins with observation – seeing every detail, like a bite mark or a bruise, and carefully noting its size, shape, colour, or other features. With laboratory tests, medical knowledge, and scientific thinking, forensic pathologists interpret those detailed clues. Their primary goal, which you'll explore in this book, is to offer detectives an expert opinion, a scientific explanation of how someone died.

"WHAT HAPPENED TO ME?"

Dr. Lester Adelson (1914– 2006, an American coroner who performed 8,000 autopsies) described autopsies as a 'dialogue with the dead'. It's true: a corpse raises questions without saying a word. The big one for a forensic pathologist is, "What happened to me?" The answer often depends on other questions:

- "Who am I?"
- "When did I die?"
- "Where did I die?"
- "Why did I die?"
- "Who killed me?"

5

A 'toe tag' lists the name, birthdate and record number of the deceased to avoid mix-ups at the morgue. Unidentified bodies are registered as 'John Doe' or 'Jane Doe'.

Dr. Mike Dobersen is a doctor whose 'patients' are dead! As the forensic pathologist of Arapahoe County, Colorado, he and his team perform 500 autopsies each year – an average of two each working day. About 25 of those autopsies involve a murder victim. Most of the other deaths are natural, followed by accidents and then suicides.

The autopsies take place in Dr. Dobersen's morgue, which has a large, chilled room where bodies are stored on rolling tables. Besides the forensic pathologist, the morgue is filled with other doctors and scientists of the dead. Their titles tend to end in '–ologist', which means 'expert': Dr. Kelly Lear-Kaul (Dr. Dobersen's colleague) is a forensic pathologist, an expert in autopsies and diseases.

Chemists called toxicologists test blood and other body samples collected by a pathologist for chemicals – natural or otherwise.

Some cases demand the dental know-how of an odontologist, like Dr. Levine who matched Ted Bundy's teeth to the bite mark on the corpse. If the body is a skeleton, an anthropologist, or bone expert, takes a look.

Add the word 'forensic' to any of these –ologist titles, and the person doubles as a crime scientist. A regular pathologist examines bodies for signs of injury or disease. A forensic pathologist, like Dr. Lear-Kaul, knows how to interpret injuries as evidence in a crime.

Dead or alive?

When a corpse is found, and there's any doubt about the death, the police call a forensic pathologist to the scene. (See 'Making the Call'.) But first, it's important to make sure the person is really dead. This might surprise you: it's not always easy.

Dr. Dobersen remembers the case of a woman found home alone in the winter in Seattle, Washington. Her house had no heat, and her body was cold to the touch. An emergency rescue team felt no pulse and so called the forensic pathologist, who couldn't feel anything either. The woman hadn't moved and didn't appear to be breathing. The woman was declared dead, and sealed in a body bag.

During the drive to the morgue, inside a heated vehicle, the bag suddenly began moving – the woman was alive! Her heart beats and breathing had been too slow and too faint to detect due to her extremely low body temperature (caused by being unconscious in a freezing house for a long period of time).

In other cases, death is all too clear.

MAKING THE CALL

Police call a forensic pathologist to a crime scene in these situations:

- Cases of violence (even if they appear to be accidents or suicides).
- A sudden death that a doctor cannot explain.
- An accidental hospital death (for example, during an operation).
- A death involving alcohol, drugs, or other toxins.
- A stillbirth or the death of a newborn baby (less than 24 hours old).
- The death of someone in prison or in police custody.
- The death of someone working on a job.
- An unidentified or unclaimed body.

7

A forensic pathologist checks and prepares the instruments that will be used to perform an autopsy.

On the case

On 20 June, 2006, detectives call Dr. Dobersen to a crime scene in Aurora, Colorado – a burned-out apartment contains the dead body of a young woman. The crime scene investigation team have spent an entire day taking photos and carefully searching the scene for evidence. But everyone knows not to touch the woman's body.

'Do not disturb' is a key rule because the position of a body can tell investigators a lot about what might have happened. Also, it is likely that any evidence taken from the body belongs to the killer or the victim. If evidence is linked to someone else, like a careless detective, it could be thrown out of the case.

POLICE LINE DO NOT CROSS

At the crime scene

Dr. Dobersen lifts the yellow tape marking off the crime scene. He walks under it into a blackened, first-floor flat.

"It's just a gutted mess," the fire chief is telling reporters. But Dr. Dobersen knows that in this mess are the clues to the killer.

Dr. Dobersen asks the detectives for the facts of the case. The detectives say the woman who lived in the flat was reported missing two days earlier. Her car was stolen and then involved in an accident. The driver was arrested.

Is the woman found in the fire the same one who is missing? Dr. Dobersen won't know for sure until he examines the body for proof of identity. But if the victim is the missing tenant, the fact that she's been gone for two days is a clue to time of death.

Examining the body

Without touching anything, a forensic photographer takes pictures of the bedroom and wardrobe where the body is lying face-down.

Dr. Dobersen observes both the young woman's wrists and ankles are tied, and there's a phone cord wrapped around her neck. The doctor is relieved to see that her hands are tied in front of her body. That means he can take fingerprints, which would have otherwise burned off. Dr. Dobersen spots a number of stab wounds and alerts detectives to look for a weapon. Sure enough, they soon find an empty space in a knife block –a kitchen knife is missing.

Crime scene investigators finalise their notes after leaving a building where a crime has been committed. They wear a one-piece paper suit with a hood and booties to stop fibres from their own clothes and hairs from contaminating the scene. While at the scene they wear gloves and a face mask.

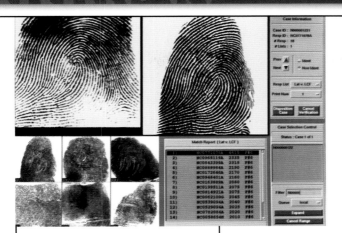

A corpse that is too badly disfigured to be identified can sometimes still give a fingerprint! If the victim has been fingerprinted in the past (following, for example, an arrest) his or her fingerprints will be on record in a computerised Automated Fingerprint Identification System (A.F.I.S.).

Sometimes, Dr. Dobersen takes the body's temperature at the scene. Since bodies gradually cool in the hours after death, temperature is a clue to when the person died. But, in this case, the hot fire has made a temperature reading worthless.

Dr. Dobersen learns that firefighters have found traces of an accelerant, an easy-burn substance such as petrol that makes flames spread quickly.

This would indicate that someone set the fire on purpose.

A crime scene photographer documents a crime scene and all the evidence before it's collected.

A CAREER IN CRIME SCIENCE PROFILE:
DR. MIKE DOBERSEN M.E.

Dr. Mike Dobersen is both a medical examiner and a forensic pathologist, but his job title is 'coroner'.

The job of coroner is a political one, not a scientific one. Every four years, Dr. Dobersen has to run for the office in an election, asking the people of Arapahoe County to vote for him.

Dr. Dobersen is qualified to perform autopsies, teach medical skills, and testify in court as an expert witness (see page 7 HELP WANTED). Dr. Dobersen also holds a double Ph.D., the highest education degree, in microbiology and biochemistry.

Dr. Dobersen started his career peering through microscopes at bacteria and viruses, researching the simplest organisms. He switched to examining human corpses for two main reasons:

"One reason is that the person may be dead, but the families are still alive", he says. "My job is to speak for the dead on behalf of the living". Another reason is that looking at and into a body is like solving a big, interesting puzzle. Dr. Dobersen never knows what mysteries and hidden clues he'll discover.

With his knowledge and skills, Dr. Dobersen can help families find out what happened to their loved one.

9

Was it the killer? And, if so, did the killer start the blaze in order to kill his or her victim, or to cover up a murder by other means. Finding the answers will take slow, careful teamwork to collect evidence in the charred ruins.

The next big question is what killed the victim. Did the victim die from strangulation or stabbing, or was she killed by the smoke or fire? After an hour at the scene, Dr. Dobersen decides it's better to do a slow, careful autopsy back at the morgue rather than try to learn anything more on site. He asks for the body to be wrapped and sent to his morgue.

Causes of death

Remember, the main goal of an autopsy is to determine the cause of death. So, how many ways can one person die at the hand of another? Unfortunately, there are many, many ways. Yet all deadly acts boil down to a biological truth: the cause of death is a lack of something vital to life, something a body needs to survive.

TYPES OF TRAUMA

Trauma to a body can be described in three ways:

- A blunt force – such as a blow to the body.
- A sharp force – such as a knife wound.
- A projectile – such as a bullet, fragments from a bomb, or other objects flung at high speed.

The most important of these is oxygen. A body can last almost a week without water (until death by dehydration) and eight to 12 weeks without food (until death by starvation). But a brain can survive for only four to six minutes without oxygen.

Dying from lack of oxygen is called asphyxia and it covers a lot of criminal ground. In a drowning, the presence of water in the lungs means there's no oxygen to breathe. Strangling, choking and smothering prevent oxygen from entering the windpipe and lungs. Crushing of the chest, as by a heavy object, keeps the lungs from expanding and drawing in air.

Some toxins can also cause death by asphyxia on a body-cell level.

Body bags are airtight and waterproof. They keep odours, body fluids, and most importantly physical evidence inside during transport to the morgue.

Carbon monoxide is a gas that spews from a car's exhaust pipe, and is created by fires. After it is inhaled, the gas molecules latch onto the haemoglobin in red blood cells, where oxygen normally hitches a ride. The oxygen molecules are left without a seat, and the person dies within minutes from asphyxia. Cyanide is a poison that blocks cells from taking in oxygen from the blood.

Trauma to vital organs

Many murders involve the failure of vital organs or the loss of too much blood. Here's where trauma – damage to the body – plays a central role. A blow, a stab wound, and a bullet can all injure the body. If these wounds cause the brain, heart, liver, or another vital organ to stop working, they're fatal.

Identity revealed

Dr. Dobersen's autopsy of the Aurora victim takes unusually long – more than three hours. Fingerprints and teeth x-rays confirm that she's the missing woman who lived in the now-burned apartment. She was a 23-year-old, African American beauty salon worker. Her name is kept secret because the case is still open at the time of this writing. More details are coming in Chapter 3. But first, here's a closer look at what death means.

When forensic pathologist Dr. Michael Hunter examined this photograph, this is what he saw: "Below the chin is a dried abrasion (injury on the skin surface). The size and shape approximate the ligature (cord) in the photo. The dried blood is from an open wound of an unknown source".

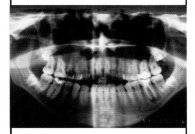

Forensic pathologists can compare an x-ray of a corpse's teeth with dental x-rays to identify an unknown person. A.D.I.S (Automated Dental Identification System) is a computer database of dental x-rays that compares an x-ray of an unknown person's teeth with a vast number of dental x-rays of known persons, looking for a match.

The forensic pathologist's main quest is to find the manner and cause of death. But, at the scene of a murder, one of the first questions the police often ask is: "When did the victim die?" In a film, an actor playing a forensic pathologist might lay a firm hand on the corpse, and say, "Three hours ago, tops. The body's still warm." But that's fiction.

Real forensic pathologists know that pinning down the time since death is a very tricky science. They rely on a handful of biological clocks – changes in the body that take place minutes, hours, and days after the moment of death. The tricky part is that no two bodies change in exactly the same way because of variables – the many factors and conditions that affect those changes.

For example, a pathologist has to consider: what is the body's mass and fat-to-muscle content? Are there any open wounds from cuts, burns, or bullets? Is the body in water or on land? Is it buried or in the open? What's the weather like – hot or cold, rainy or dry?

Still, even with all the variables, corpses change over time according to basic laws of science. And a pathologist knows those laws inside and out.

Minutes to hours

At the moment of death, all the body's systems shut down. Brain cells no longer send electrical signals to each other and begin dying off very quickly. The lungs stop pulling in air and pushing out carbon dioxide. The blood stops circulating immediately, causing the skin to turn pale. Muscles, including the heart, no longer contract, and so become limp. Muscle cells die more slowly than brain cells, since they depend less on oxygen.

A key standstill, from a crime-solving point of view, is the digestive system. The stomach and intestines stop breaking down food. During an autopsy, if the pathologist finds fresh-looking chunks of meat and potatoes in the stomach, then the person probably died soon after eating. If police know when that last meal took place, the pathologist counts forward to the

The crime team on the TV drama *CSI: Crime Scene Investigation* ponders whether this woman died from an accidental fall in the episode 'Bite Me'. The show's forensic pathologist, Doc Robbins, doubts it: "If my full autopsy confirms murder, you may be looking at the first serial stairway killer".

This black hole is a cross-section of a blood vessel in a brain. The red dots are neurons (nerve cells). And the green blotches? They're glial cells, which help deliver nutrition and oxygen from the blood to the neurons, among many other duties.

time of death, give or take a couple hours. (See ON THE CASE: A Stomach for Murder? on page 15.)

Meanwhile, every body, dead or alive, teems with bacteria. A corpse no longer has a working immune system – natural defences – and so these hungry microbes are suddenly free to attack. The bacteria consume body cells and expel gases as waste products, causing the corpse to swell up and bloat in the first few days. Those gases are what produce the very strong, distinct, and rotten odour of human death. The amount of decomposition – how much

of the body has broken down – is a general clue to time of death. Fortunately, there are three better body clocks that start ticking the moment life ends. A pathologist can use them to estimate when a 'fresh' corpse, one that's a couple of days old, was killed.

YOUR BRAIN ON OXYGEN

You know the process:

• Your lungs breathe in air.

• The oxygen latches on to haemoglobin in the blood.

• The blood circulates all around your body.

• One fourth of that oxygen ends up in your brain cells, which quickly use the gas to make chemicals.

Your brain cells can't hold more than 10 seconds worth of oxygen at a time. That's why, in cases of asphyxia (lack of oxygen), the brain is usually the first organ to die.

Within moments, the 'cold hand of death' turns skin of all tones (dark or light) a paler shade as red blood cells lose oxygen and break down.

On the TV show *CSI: NY*, the lead characters Mac and Stella check out the body of a man who bled to death in the snow. Cold temperatures speed up algor mortis (body cooling) but slow down rigor mortis (muscle stiffening) and decomposition.

The mortis clocks

Crime films aren't totally wrong: dead bodies can no longer heat themselves, and so they gradually match the ambient temperature – the temperature of the place that they're in. That change is called *algor mortis*, Latin for 'cold death'. It's one of three basic biological clocks for estimating time of death in a new corpse.

All things being average, a corpse drops less than half a degree (Celsius) per hour over the first six hours and reaches the ambient temperature by about 12 to 18 hours.

The trouble is, all things are never average. Clothing or other coverings slow down cooling. Children and thinner people cool off faster than adults and heavy people because they have less mass. Water saps heat from a body faster than air does.

A normal body temperature at death is 37°C, but some victims might be hotter or, in a case of hypothermia, much cooler. Body temperature can even rise after death!

How? Don't forget those busy bacteria: decomposition is a chemical process that generates heat. Also, in a hot desert or in the Tropics or near a fire, the ambient temperature can be higher than 37°C. The body temperature will rise to meet it.

The second biological clock, *livor mortis* ('blue death'), is about blood and gravity. Blood is no longer being pumped around the body, and so gravity takes over. Suppose a body is lying flat on its back. Blood flows slowly to the lowest points – in this case, the backside. It pools in places that aren't in hard contact with a surface such as the back of the neck and thighs and the curved part of the lower back. Pink dots and blotches appear within about a half hour to an hour after death. The pink darkens to red, and then slowly to purplish blue, as oxygen escapes from the blood.

In the first few hours after death, these bruise-like stains spread and meet up. They turn white when touched and are still fluid. Then, roughly 10 hours after death, they darken.

ON THE CASE:

A STOMACH FOR MURDER?

The last meal David Hendricks and his three children shared together was a pizza topped with mushrooms, black olives, green peppers, tomatoes, and onions. On 7 November, 1983, the kids gulped down the pizza slices at a restaurant in Bloomington, Illinois.

Later that night, at around midnight, Hendricks drove out of town on a business trip. The next night, police found his wife, Susan, and the children, aged five, seven, and nine, dead in their beds. The murder weapons, an old axe and a knife, had been wiped clean of fingerprints. In fact, detectives found no direct evidence pointing to a killer.

TIME OF DEATH

Autopsies revealed that the children still had pizza toppings in their stomachs. It takes two to four hours for a meal to move into the intestines. Since the kids had eaten at 7 p.m., that meant they were probably killed between 9 and 11 p.m. – while their father was still at home. Hendricks was put on trial for murdering his family. Dr. Michael Baden, M.E., told the court that the mushrooms, black olives, and onions looked so fresh that the murder was probably closer to 9 p.m. than 11 p.m. The defence pointed out the children ate quickly so they could go to the restaurant's play area; gulping and exercise slow down digestion. Not by that much, Dr. Baden countered. He stuck to his two hour estimate.

THE VERDICTS

David Hendricks was found guilty. Then, in 1990, a court overturned that verdict and awarded him a second trial. The new jury found Hendricks not guilty! The medical evidence hadn't changed. The difference was that these jurors believed the time of death wasn't very clear. With no direct evidence against Hendricks, they had too much doubt to convict him.

As in sports and entertainment, crime science has its superstars. Dr. Michael Baden is a 'celebrity' forensic pathologist drawn to high-profile cases like the Hendricks murder and the assassinations of President John F. Kennedy and Dr. Martin Luther King, Jr.

TIMETABLE OF LIVIDITY

Lividity, the low spots where blood pools, changes in colour over time:

- Pink: about 15 to 30 minutes after death.
- Blue-purple: about 1 to 3 hours after death.
- Purple-red: about 6 to 8 hours after death.

Why a corpse is a stiff

The third biological clock, which 'ticks' for two or three days after death, is *rigor mortis* ('rigid death'). It's the reason a corpse is nicknamed a 'stiff'. One to two hours after death, the smallest muscles, starting in the jaw and face, contract and stay that way, as if made of stone. Over several hours, the stiffening spreads to larger muscles – the limbs – and then, at about 10 hours, the hips. At 12 hours, give or take, the body enters full rigor: every muscle stiff as a board. It looks and feels like a statue.

Muscles lock into place like this because a corpse can no longer produce a chemical called ATP (adenosine triphosphate). A body that is low in ATP at death enters into and goes through rigor mortis faster. (ATP levels drop during energetic exercise or an intense physical struggle.) Warm weather also speeds up the muscle stiffening; cold weather slows it. As with the other two biological clocks, the timing is never exactly the same.

Bacteria and the body's own enzymes decompose the muscles, breaking down the stiff tissue. Enzymes are proteins that body cells make to trigger chemical actions such as the digestion of food. In effect, a dead body slowly digests itself as enzymes spread unchecked! The muscles begin to soften and loosen up in reverse order, from larger to smaller until, finally, the jaw muscles go limp. This reversal can take anything from one to three days.

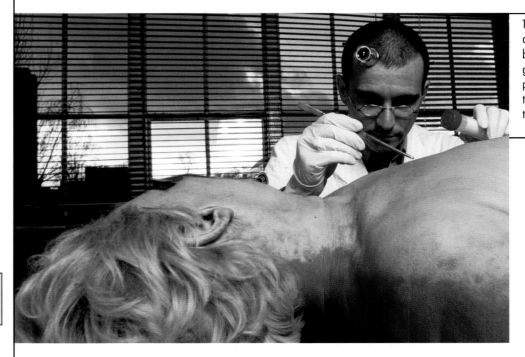

The blood inside this corpse pooled on the backside, thanks to gravity. The lividity pattern stays fixed; touching or turning over the body won't change it.

ON THE CASE:

WHEN BODY CLOCKS DISAGREE: PART 1

John Belushi was a comic actor. He was also a drug addict. Belushi's death, on 5 March, 1982, presented forensic pathologists with a time-of-death puzzle.

The manner of death wasn't a murder. It was an accident – an overdose of drugs. But his drug supplier, Cathy Smith, was arrested for murder. Estimating Belushi's time of death was a key factor in deciding her guilt or innocence.

Below is the timeline of events. It includes observations about the three mortis clocks – algor mortis (temperature), livor mortis (blood pooling), and rigor mortis (muscle stiffening). Can you make sense of the observations to estimate a time of death?

Timetable of death – 5 March, 1982

3:00 a.m. John Belushi ends a four-day, drug-taking party by announcing that he's cold and wants to be alone. Everyone leaves except Cathy Smith.

3:30 a.m. Smith gives Belushi a shot of drugs and then turns up the heater, after he complains again of being cold.

10:15 a.m. Smith leaves the apartment while, she says, Belushi is alive and sleeping.

12:30 p.m. An exercise trainer finds Belushi dead.

12:35 p.m. Paramedics arrive and note that Belushi's jaw is stiff, a first sign of rigor mortis. (Rigor sets in roughly one to two hours after death.)

4:37 p.m. The coroner examines the body at the scene. He notes that the reddish-purple spots of livor mortis blanch (turn white) when touched. (This normally happens about 6 to 8 hours after death.) The body temperature is 35°C. Remember that at room temperature, it normally drops roughly 1-2 degrees per hour for the first six hours.)

As you can see, sometimes it's not easy! What do you think was the most likely time of death?

Turn the page to read the expert opinion of Dr. Michael Baden, M.E...

Comedians John Belushi (left) and Dan Ackroyd played the ultra-cool Jake and Elwood Blues in the 1980 film *The Blues Brothers*.

ON THE CASE:

WHEN BODY CLOCKS DISAGREE: PART 2
(continued from page 17)

So...about what time did John Belushi die of a drug overdose? Dr. Michael Baden M.E. noted that Belushi's body temperature of 35°C would normally put death at around 1 p.m. This was after the body was found. Impossible!

THE M.E'.S CONCLUSION

The two other biological clocks gave different answers. Dr. Baden said the rigor mortis in the jaw suggested a range of 10:30 to 11:30 a.m., which is just after Smith left the apartment. The blanching of livor mortis put death between 8:30 to 10:30 a.m. – before Smith left. Dr. Baden concluded that the most likely time of death was close to 10:30 a.m., when the algor and rigor observations overlap. He also concluded that the body temperature was unusually high for a couple of reasons: although Belushi complained of feeling cold, Dr. Baden said the actor probably had a slight fever caused by heavy drug use. His body temperature started a few degrees above 37°C. Then, after death, his corpse took longer than normal to cool because of physics: the greater the body mass, the slower the loss of heat. John Belushi was a large man.

THE VERDICT

The toxicology report showed a large amount of drugs in the body. That fact pointed to a second shot, probably given to Belushi at about 8:30 a.m., or two hours before the estimated time of death. Cathy Smith was the only person present to give this fatal dose. She agreed to plead guilty to the less serious charge of involuntary manslaughter.

John Belushi's body is removed from a bungalow at the Chateau Marmont Hotel in Los Angeles, California, 5 March, 1982. He was 33 years old at the time of his death.

Together, the three mortis clocks – algor, livor, and rigor – allow a pathologist to give a range for time of death that's a couple of hours at best and usually wider. A small percentage of bodies will always fall outside this range, so the pathologist never says, "This person died at such-and-such time." It's more like, "The most likely time of death is between three and six hours ago, but I can never be 100 percent sure." To blur the lines further, the three biological clocks sometimes aren't even in sync with each other. (See ON THE CASE: When Body Clocks Disagree page 17.)

What happens after the body reaches the ambient temperature? After lividity is fixed? After rigor mortis sets in and sets out? For bodies dead more than a few days, pathologists look elsewhere for time-of-death clues.

Long-term changes

The Body Farm is a place full of human bodies. It's not a morgue or a graveyard or the scene of a horrible mass murder. It's a scientific centre for researching how bodies decompose over days, weeks, and months. The bodies were donated to science by their previous owners.

The Body Farm's real name is the Anthropology Research Center at the University of Tennessee in the US. Like murder victims, the experimental bodies are put in a variety of situations: buried in soil, left in the open air, sunk in water, locked in a car boot, set into concrete, and so on.

Scientists check them often and carefully. They take photos, measure the ambient temperature and the body temperature, collect gases from decomposition, test the soil for chemical changes, and take samples of body tissue to test and examine in a lab.

Over a couple of months, a body in water can develop 'grave wax', a waxy, white solid called adipocere. This forms because fatty acids in the

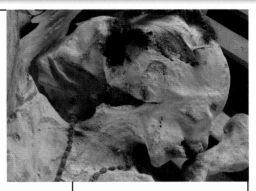

This ghostly-looking corpse was one of half a million or so people murdered in Rwanda, Africa, in the spring of 1994. The white coating is a natural, soaplike 'grave wax' that forms when the body's fatty acids mix with alkaline (non-acidic) water.

At the Body Farm in Tennessee, scientists exhume (dig up) and photograph a corpse that has been buried specifically to see how the body decomposes.

Bluebottle larvae are just one of the many insects that feed on the corpses let out in the open at the Body Farm.

19

corpse react with alkaline (non-acidic) chemicals – the same process by which soap is made. Even when adipocere doesn't form, a body introduces fatty acids to the soil. The amount of fatty acids, when adjusted for changes in ambient temperature, is yet another clue to time of death.

In a very dry environment, the rotting process slows or stops. Corpses can turn into natural mummies, their skin and flesh tough and dry, like leather. But Tennessee is generally warm and wet for most of the year.

Warm, moist flesh rots down to the skeleton quickly, thanks to a parade of decomposers. These bacteria, flies, ants, beetles, and other insects feed on dead plant and animal tissue. Their order of arrival and the life cycles of the insects – from egg to adult – are surprisingly good clues to time of death. (See *ON THE CASE: Timed Flies*, right.)

In the late stages of decomposition, weeks and months after death, the organs and flesh break down into a liquid state and drain away from the body. The body's own enzymes help this process along.

Controlled experiments, like those at the Body Farm, help sharpen and narrow all the time-of-death estimates. Detailed charts can be produced of data – hourly temperatures, chemical contents, numbers and types and sizes of decomposers,

Blowflies often invade a dead body within minutes; this blowfly larva is feeding on a liver. Other decomposers show up after the chemistry of corpse changes to their liking. House flies might be followed by beetles that eat fly larvae, and then by egg-laying wasps. When all the liquid is gone, mites set in.

and so on. When faced with a murder mystery, forensic pathologists and other crime scientists use these careful measures as a guide.

They still can't say 'when', exactly. But in some cases 'about when' is close enough to catch a killer.

Like the ancient Egyptians, the Guanche people of the Canary Islands near West Africa knew how to turn bodies into mummies by stopping decomposition. They removed the organs, dried the corpses in the sun, and then wrapped them in animal skins.

20

ON THE CASE:

TIMED FLIES

On 29 May, 1984, nine-year-old Vernita Wheat of Wisconsin, US, disappeared with a family friend. Her mother knew this adult 'friend' as Robert until she found his photo in a police mug book under the name 'Alton Coleman'. She learned to her horror, that Coleman was a violent criminal soon to make the FBI's 'Most Wanted' list.

On 19 June, police discovered Vernita's badly decomposed body in a boarded-up building. The key question was: when did she die? Was she strangled soon after disappearing, which would cast a dark shadow of guilt on Coleman? Or did she die days later, perhaps at the cruel hands of someone else?

THE INVESTIGATION

The body and room were teeming with insects. The crime scene investigation team collected samples at four stages in a fly's life cycle:

1. fat, white, wormlike maggots (advanced larvae)
2. pupae inside hard, brown cases
3. newly hatched flies
4. dead adult flies

Bernard Greenberg, a forensic entomologist (insect expert), identified most of the insects as black blow flies, with a life cycle of 14 to 17 days from egg to adult. This species was no help, since Vernita had disappeared 20 days earlier.

THE BREAKTHROUGH

Then, on 30 June, a month after she vanished, more of the pupae cases broke open. Out came bluebottle flies, with a life cycle from egg to adult of 33 days – when kept at 15°C. Cold temperatures slow down growth. So Greenberg checked the hourly weather reports for the past month. Using a calculator, he subtracted time from the 33-day life cycle for each hour that was very chilly. His backward calculations stopped at midnight, when 29 May turned into 30 May.

Bluebottles are active in daylight, so Greenberg worked out the flies laid their eggs on the girl's body at dawn on 30 May. Vernita died less than a day after she disappeared!

Based on Greenberg's 'fly time' and other indirect evidence, Alton Coleman was found guilty of her murder – and, in other cases, of seven other murders. In 2002, he was put to death by the state of Ohio.

An adult body holds about 5 litres of blood. The raised edges of an autopsy table keep all that liquid from flowing onto the floor.

The corpse of the Aurora, Colorado, victim arrives in the office of Dr. Mike Dobersen, M.E., in a sealed bag. Several bags, actually. At the crime scene, the feet and hands were bagged to secure any bits of evidence that might fall off. The body bag is always a fresh, new one, to avoid mixing in evidence from another case. A separate bag holds the victim's burned clothing. This will also be carefully examined for evidence.

Dr. Dobersen always breaks the seals of the bags in front of witnesses – two detectives, in this case, who stay for the whole autopsy. The presence of witnesses prevents someone from later claiming the body was tampered with between the crime scene and the morgue.

The pathologist works very slowly and carefully with his two morgue attendants. He doesn't want to miss an important detail or, worse, make a mistake that ruins evidence for use at trial.

Preparing the body

For each autopsy, the attendants and a forensic photographer have plenty of work to do: the body

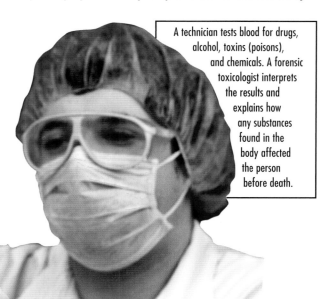

A technician tests blood for drugs, alcohol, toxins (poisons), and chemicals. A forensic toxicologist interprets the results and explains how any substances found in the body affected the person before death.

is photographed, still in the opened bag, and then at every stage of the autopsy. Blood, urine, and other samples are collected and sent to the toxicology lab. So are any bits of dirt or plant matter, or other trace evidence found on the body.

Fingerprints are taken, which, in this case, help identify the victim as the 23-year-old beauty salon worker who lived in the apartment and was reported missing. Close-up photos are taken of any scars, tattoos, bruises, wounds, and other marks on the body. The corpse is also x-rayed, weighed, and, finally, cleaned.

The attendants place the body face-up on a slightly slanted, metal table with grooves along the side edges. The grooves allow fluids to drain away. An attendant places a small block under the subject's back, between the shoulders, to make the chest stick up and the head and arms fall back.

The corpse is now ready to be examined outside, and in.

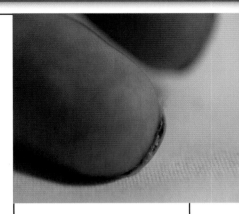

The pathologist can collect a bounty of trace evidence under the victim's fingernails. Fibres and dirt are clues to the location of the crime. If a victim scratched the attacker, the murderer's skin cells or blood might be present (as seen in this photograph). Both materials contain DNA that can be used to identify the killer.

THE AUTOPSY TOOL KIT

Instruments used for surgery are usually fine, special tools for making careful cuts and doing as little damage as possible to the body. Autopsy tools are heavy-duty, and designed to get the job done efficiently and quickly.

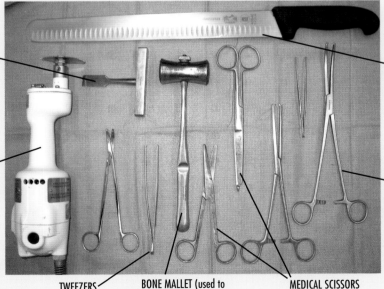

SKULL BREAKER (used to open up skull sections)

STRYKER SAW (used to cut through the skull)

BREAD KNIFE (used for cutting thin slices of organs)

FORCEPS (large tweezers used for lifting organs from the body)

TWEEZERS

BONE MALLET (used to chisel off pieces of bone)

MEDICAL SCISSORS

WHAT CAN WOUNDS MEAN?

- A bullet hole in the skin is either an entrance wound or an exit wound. These two entrance wounds are close contact gunshot wounds. The one on the left shows an abrasion (skin injury) that matches the shape of the gun tip. The one on the right has a soot mark. During the autopsy, the forensic pathologist traces the path of the bullet through the body.

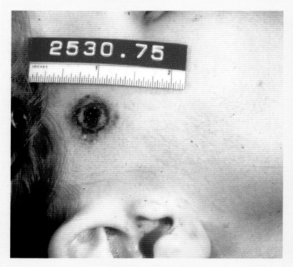

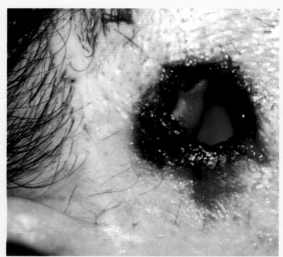

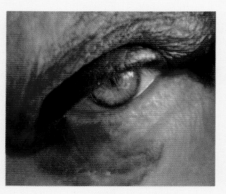

- Contusions, or bruises (left), form when blunt force trauma breaks the blood vessels. The colour of a bruise changes from red to purple to brown to green to yellow. This can be a clue to the time of injury. Corpses are no longer pumping blood, so they don't get bruised. A blunt force trauma injury, with no bruising, happened at, or after death.

- A haemorrhage is uncontrolled bleeding. It can be external or internal. An injury without haemorrhaging took place after death, when the heart was no longer pumping blood.

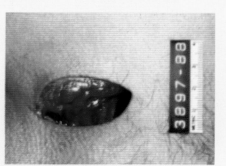

- This stab wound (left) has very sharp edges and corners with no abrasions or contusions on the surrounding skin, as happens with blunt force trauma. It's an incision wound (a cut) rather than a laceration, which is a tear in tissue due to an impact such as a hammer blow.

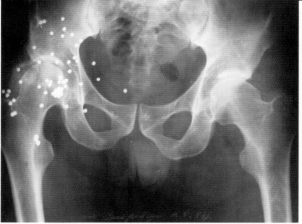

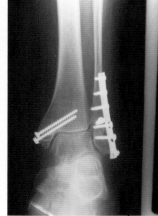

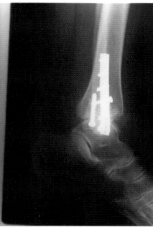

The external exam

With a recently dead corpse, forensic pathologists take note of two of the three mortis clocks: They observe the colour, location, and state of lividity – blanching or fixed – and they bend the joints to check for rigor mortis. (A body temperature reading is useless, since the corpse is refrigerated before the autopsy.)

Forensic pathologists also look for unusual skin colouring. A recent corpse is normally a paler version of its living self. Green or marbled, veiny-looking skin are clues to the stage of decomposition. Marbling happens as bacteria travel freely through blood vessels and darken their colour. These changes happen to people of all skin colours, dark or light, because they aren't related to melanin, the pigment that determines skin tone.

In this case, the woman's body is too badly burned to make most of these observations possible. Talking into a recorder, Dr. Dobersen examines the body from head to toe, describing in detail the external evidence of murder. He finds:

- *Severe burns on the left shoulder and left side of the face (the parts closest to the fire).*

- *Only a small amount of burn damage on her front (she was lying face down).*

- *A ligature mark around the neck and ligatures around the ankles and wrists. (The cords are removed during body prep and examined as evidence.)*

- *Seven sharp-force injuries (cuts) that are consistent with knife wounds.*

Dr. Dobersen checks the area around the burned skin for a vital reaction – any swelling that means blood cells had started to repair the wounds. There is no swelling, which is one sign that the woman was dead before the fire. Another sign is a lack of soot in her airway: she didn't breathe in any smoke. Sometimes, the doctor uses his nose to sniff out

X-rays both reveal and document hidden evidence, like the pattern of gunshot fragments in this man's hip (left). They also provide clues to an unknown person's identity. For example, the metal pins in the ankles (centre) can be matched to medical records.

During an autopsy, the pathologist's hands are busy, bloody, and rubber-gloved. So, instead of writing notes, it's easier to dictate observations into a voice-activated recorder.

clues, especially if he suspects toxins might be present. A fire can release cyanide into the air, along with carbon monoxide, as it burns certain materials. Cyanide smells like bitter almonds to some people, but like rotten cabbage to Dr. Dobersen. This time, he doesn't smell anything unusual, though. A lab test will later show that there's no carbon monoxide attached to the haemoglobin in the woman's blood.

Dr. Dobersen rules out fire as the cause of death and turns his careful attention to her other injuries.

Cords and cuts

A cord was found around the woman's neck. Was she strangled? If so, her capillaries, the tiniest blood vessels, probably burst in her eyes, eyelids, and perhaps her face. This creates tiny, red speckles called petechiae. Dr. Dobersen doesn't see any.

Another sign of strangulation is a broken hyoid bone – a U-shaped bone in the front of the neck. It can crack under pressure, but this woman's hyoid bone is intact. Dr. Dobersen doubts that she was strangled to death. That leaves the lacerations.

He measures every stab wound very precisely. He labels the seven lacerations from A to G, records their maximum length and width, their exact position on the body, and any other features. In the films, forensic pathologists somehow match a stab wound exactly with a murder weapon. In real life, that's pretty much impossible to do in soft tissue – like skin and flesh and organs.

Dr. Dobersen remembers one of his cases in which forensic anthropologist, Dr. Diane France,

The most common autopsy cut is Y-shaped, with the two prongs of the 'Y' starting at the shoulders.

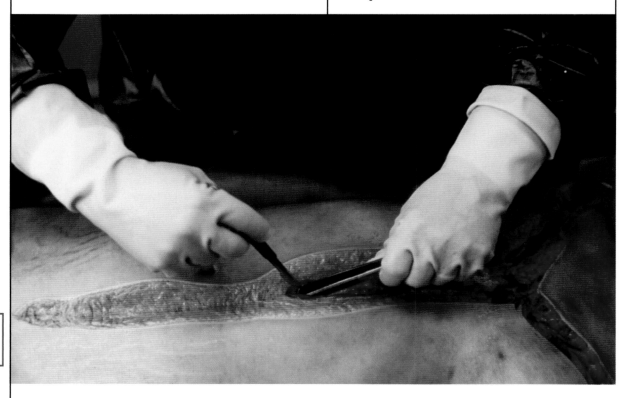

made an exact, and rare, match between an injury and a weapon. Dr. France found a clear knife mark in the victim's cartilage, the white, bony cushion at the joints. She likened it to sticking a blade in extra-firm jelly and pulling it out cleanly. The mark, she noted, was made by a blade with a broken tip. The killer had bragged about just such a weapon, his 'favourite knife'. The braggart was convicted of murder.

For the case at hand, Dr. Dobersen notes into his recorder that most of the woman's stab wounds look superficial (not very deep), but he can't really tell from the outside. It's time to trace the path of each one to see where it leads.

Inside the body

Using a large scalpel, Dr. Dobersen makes deep cuts from each

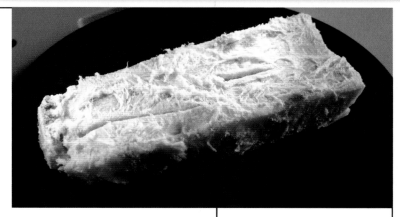

shoulder down to the bottom of the torso. The pattern is a Y, or a U with a tail at the bottom, and so this classic autopsy cut is called a Y- or U-incision. It allows the pathologist to lift up a broad flap of flesh and muscle and fold it up, over the face, exposing the ribs and organs.

Dr. Dobersen spots a tool mark on the rib cage. The likely murder weapon, a kitchen knife, is missing. With this mark left in

Bones are called 'hard tissue', but they're softer than metal, and so a knife blade makes tool marks in them. The scrape mark (upper right) and long slice (lower left) on this bone are clues to the size and shape of the murder weapon.

Does this human heart look healthy to you? Other than having been sliced in half, it's 'unremarkable'. That's the autopsy word for 'normal'. The pathologist weighs and dissects organs separately in the search for a condition, colour, or size that's not normal.

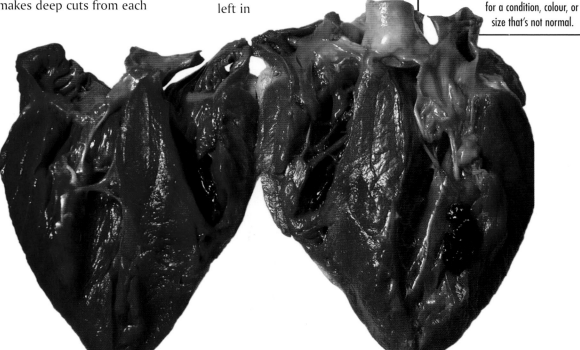

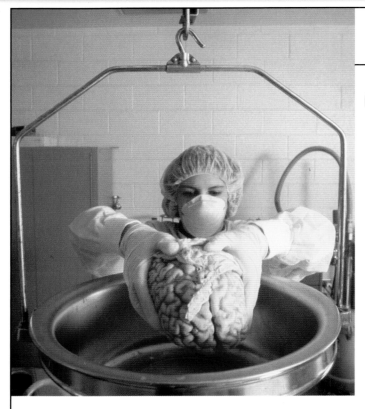

Organs that weigh too much or too little could be diseased or injured, especially if their colour or texture is off, too. A healthy adult brain weighs about 1150 to 1450 grams.

like taking off a hood in reverse. Next, he saws a circle around the top of the skull and pries off the cap of bone. The brain is examined, taken out, and weighed.

A swollen brain is a sign of injury before death – again, the body's defences rushing to repair a wound. If it's not swollen, any injuries probably happened after death. The doctor finds no evidence of murder in the brain.

Finally, Dr. Dobersen sews the body back together, using a long, heavy needle and thick, waxed thread. When all the results come back in a few weeks, he will file an autopsy report for the detectives investigating the case. The report will describe all the body's organs and systems along with the injuries. It will give the doctor's interpretation of those injuries, and, most importantly, plainly state the manner and cause of death. Dr. Dobersen concludes that the manner of death was murder, and that the 23-year-old beautician died from sharp force trauma – a fatal knife wound to the heart.

hard bone, it might be possible to describe the size and type of knife – a 'class match', which describes the class, or category, of weapon used. The doctor cuts out the rib cage, frees the organs from all their attachments, and lifts them out in a block. Each one is weighed and examined separately to look for clues.

The doctor confirms that six wounds are, indeed, superficial. They haven't damaged any vital organs. One blow, however, entered he heart and was fatal. Dr. Dobersen has found the cause of death.

Wrapping it up

With the abdominal examination complete, Dr. Dobersen turns his attention to the head. He slices the flesh from ear to ear straight across the back of the head. He lifts the top section up, over the head, and onto the face,

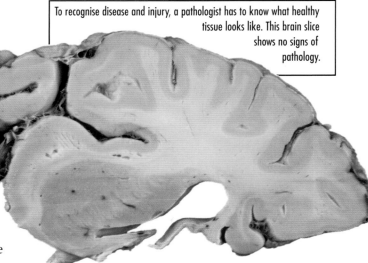

To recognise disease and injury, a pathologist has to know what healthy tissue looks like. This brain slice shows no signs of pathology.

ON THE CASE:

DROWNING IN DOUBT

Drowning is one of the hardest causes of death to prove. The mysterious case of Robert Maxwell is a good example. He was the rags-to-riches head of a publishing empire. In November 1991, the crew of his yacht reported the millionaire missing. The next day, his body was found floating in the Atlantic Ocean. Was it an accident, a suicide, or a murder? In other words, did he fall overboard, did he jump, or was he pushed?

The 45-page autopsy report, prepared by Dr. Carlos Lopez, raised more questions than it answered. It listed the manner of death as an accident, and the cause of death as heart failure. Maxwell had heart and lung damage, no question. However, other experts argue that there was no medical proof that this was what killed him.

Dr. Bernard Knight, a forensic pathologist, looked over the autopsy report and other evidence. He insists that both manner and cause are 'unascertained' (impossible to know) based on the forensic pathologist's findings.

Drowning is tough to prove, and yet it's easy to define: a lack of oxygen caused by the nose and mouth being in liquid – usually water. Like other forms of asphyxia, it's quick; it takes four to six minutes for the brain to die.

But there's no telltale medical clue that points only to drowning.

Drowning does leave medical footprints inside a body. The problem is, each of these clues can apply to causes of death other than drowning:

Fluid in the lungs and white froth in the mouth are both also present in heart failure, head injury, and drug overdose. Bloated lungs are also a sign of lung disease. Bleeding in the middle ear can also be caused by head trauma, death by electrical shock, and strangulation.

For every drowning case, the pathologist first has to determine if the victim was alive when he or she entered the water. In Robert Maxwell's case, Dr. Lopez admits that he couldn't say one way or the other. Next, the pathologist has to rule out all other possible causes of death other than drowning: hypothermia (low body temperature), trauma injuries suffered on land or in the water, and heart failure (sometimes caused by the cold shock of hitting the water).

In other words, drowning is a cause of death by default. Only a witness or a killer's confession can say for sure.

orensic pathologists search for clues in the soft tissues of the body. They look at the skin, the muscles, the organs, and even individual cells under a microscope. But what happens when a corpse is nothing but a skeleton – all bones and no flesh or blood?

'Reading' bones for clues is the work of forensic anthropologists, nicknamed 'bone detectives'. Their goal is also to determine manner and cause of death. But, when presented with a faceless, nameless skeleton, another question often moves to centre stage: "Who am I?"

Think about it. No friend or relative could recognise a skull without a face.

With a skeleton, there are no fingerprints, scars, or tattoos for identification, although sometimes clothing and jewellery found with the body can provide clues.

If the bones have fractures or odd features, forensic anthropologists could match the injuries against medical and dental x-rays. The problem is, they would need a name in order to locate those medical records.

Then there is DNA – the genetic material that makes every one of us each unique. DNA is in every body cell (except red blood cells), but it's often destroyed along with the flesh, especially in older corpses. Even if DNA is present, it can't be matched to an individual unless the person has a DNA sample on file. That's not always the case.

So how do forensic anthropologists 'read' and identify unknown bones?

> The skeleton, which includes the teeth, is the most durable part of the body. Bones can last for millions of years, as dinosaur fans well know. The human skull above is 2,000 years old, but it looks about as sharp as the modern one to the left.

HOW TO READ BONES

Are the bones male or female?

• Forensic anthropologists look primarily at the pelvis. Women give birth to babies, and so their hip bones are wider (left to right), shorter (top to bottom), and shallower (front to back) than male hips. The opening in the centre is also larger.

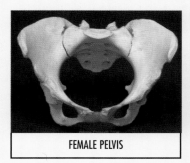
FEMALE PELVIS

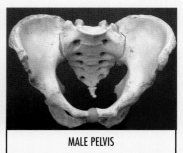
MALE PELVIS

What is the skeleton's ancestry?

• Ancestry refers to the geographic origin (Asia, Africa, or Europe for example) of a person's ancestors (forebearers). People of the same ancestry share certain skeletal features. But keep in mind, not everyone in a group has every feature and many people have mixed ancestry.

MALE EUROPEAN SKULL
People of European descent tend to have narrow skulls with sharp features, a narrow nasal passage and eyes that tend to be closer together.

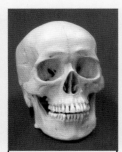
MALE ASIAN SKULL
An Asian skull is likely to have a relatively flat face, cheek bones that stick out, round eye sockets and a nasal passage that is medium in width.

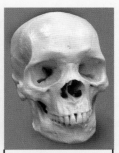
MALE AFRICAN SKULL
In this African-origin skull, the lower part of the face sticks out slightly, the eye sockets are more square-shaped, and the nasal passage is broad.

Hold old are the teeth?

• Baby teeth drop out and permanent ones grow in at a somewhat predictable rate. This can provide another clue to age. The last teeth to grow in, molars or wisdom teeth, erupt in the late teens or 20s. After that last stage is complete, forensic anthropologists look at the amount of wear and tear to estimate a broad range for an adult's age.

Hold old are the bones?

• Adults have 206 bones, but babies are born with many more. Bones fuse (or grow together) in stages until the early 20s. The amount of fusing is a general clue to age, usually given as a range of years.

MISSING PERSONS

Forensic anthropologist Clea Koff started a group called Missing Persons Identification Resource Center (MPID). It is based in California.

- There are about 100,000 missing people in the United States and about 40,000 unnamed bodies currently stored in U.S. morgues.

- The goal of MPID is to put names to those thousands of bodies. Working with the families, MPID's anthropologists develop forensic profiles for missing persons using dental and medical x-rays and DNA samples from relatives.

Who are you?

Bone detectives can't always put a name to a skeleton. But they can observe certain features, make careful measurements, and learn a person's general identity. Based on bones alone, they can identify whether the skeleton is male or female, its ancestry, and an age range (see HOW TO READ BONES on page 31). Bones can also give information about height and pathology (disease or injury). A height range is based on careful measurements of the femur (thigh bone) and sometimes the humerus (upper arm bone). Two examples of pathology include broken bones that have healed and childbirth, which leaves a distinct mark on the pelvis.

Except for pathology, very rarely does one observation or measurement point to an identifier. Bone detectives look at all the features as a whole and compare them to data collected from millions of identified skeletons. They then conclude what is the most likely answer for each identifier, as in "99 percent of skeletons with these features are women". The height and age are always given as ranges, such as 152 cm to 165 cm, or 15 to 17 years. Scientists keep in mind that a small number of cases will always fall outside the range.

A pathologist is cutting very thin slices of bone — one-tenth the thickness of this page. She'll examine the slices under a microscope for signs of disease. For example, malnutrition (poor diet) weakens bone tissue, causing it to look porous — peppered with holes where bone cells should be.

A CAREER IN CRIME SCIENCE
PROFILE: CLEA KOFF – FORENSIC ANTHROPOLOGIST

Clea Koff sorts loose bones into individual skeletons on an autopsy table. In a mass grave, that jigsaw puzzle task is sometimes impossible. As remains decay and break apart, bones can become hopelessly jumbled.

Clea Koff is both British and American. She was born in England to an American father and a mother from Tanzania, a large country in Africa. As a child, Clea took an early and unusual interest in bodies, collecting dead birds and burying them. Around the age of 13, after studying anthropology, Clea realised, "I knew that dead things could turn into bones but didn't know when or how." So she continued burying birds, but then later dug them up to see how the tiny corpses had decomposed over time.

At the age of 18, she read a true story that changed her life: Clyde Snow, a famous forensic anthropologist, wrote about digging-up mass graves in Argentina. During the mid-1970s to early 1980s, the military leaders of this South American nation had killed thousands of people. The government tried to keep it a secret, but the bones 'talked' to the science team and people were convicted of murder. Clea became instantly hooked on the idea of using science know-how to bring murderers to justice. Clea earned an anthropology degree from Stanford University in California. Then she worked in a forensic pathologist's office in Arizona, examining skeletons, while studying for an advanced college degree. That's when she was called to Rwanda, in January 1996, the first of several mass grave investigations she would undertake.

Handling a grave full of bodies is tough, tiring, and dirty work. Clea says she isn't sure she has the stamina (the staying power) to do it again, but she says, "The desire is always there."

A black feather and a long, strong beak: This skull belonged to a crow.

The number of Rwandans killed in 1994 will never be known. Estimates based on evidence found in mass graves, eyewitness accounts, and written records range from half a million to 800,000 or more.

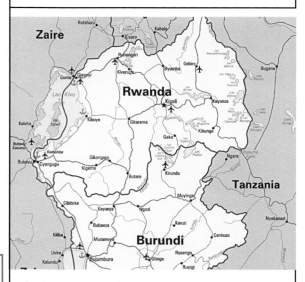

Before the 1994 genocide, the highest concentration of Tutsis in Rwanda was in the remote city of Kibuye near the western border.

Digging into mass graves

Most forensic anthropologists tackle one set of bones at a time, for example a skeleton that a hiker finds in the woods. Clea Koff investigates mass graves, scenes of horror where scores of people have been killed and buried together. She has worked at sites in Bosnia, Croatia, and Kosovo in Europe. But her first mission, in January 1996, took her back to Africa, the continent where she spent part of her childhood and where her mother, from Tanzania, was born.

Just 23-years-old, Clea flew to the country of Rwanda with 15 other doctors and expert scientists from a group called Physicians for Human Rights (PHR). The PHR team included doctors, forensic pathologists, pathologists, forensic anthropologists, archaeologists, and autopsy assistants from seven countries.

Their goal was to collect evidence of the world's worst type of crime: genocide – the killing of vast numbers of people who belong to a certain group.

Between April and July 1994, Hutus killed at least half a million Tutsis and other people who didn't go along with the killing. Half a million murders in just four months! Hutus and Tutsis are ethnic groups who share a language, a religion, and a country (Rwanda) but were separated by class, money, and power. Government and military leaders rallying for 'Hutu Power' openly called for the mass murders of Tutsis on the radio.

At one church complex of buildings in Kibuye, Clea and the PHR team dug up 493 bodies, out of perhaps 4,000 to 6,000 people killed there. It was the biggest mass grave investigation to date. A handful of friends and relatives identified the clothing, jewellery, house keys, ID cards, and other person items of their loved ones. Only 16 out of the 493 victims could be named. The rest remained identified only by case number, location of the body, and physical traits. Why?

Clea points out that, in many cases, whole families were killed – men, women, and children.

No one was left to identify victims, provide DNA samples, or give pre-death medical information. If you know someone had broken a leg, for example, you can look for a healed fracture as a clue to identification. All the scientists had were the bodies themselves.

What the bones said

The accused leaders of the genocide were about to go on trial in a world court. To convict them, the lawyers needed proof, first, that a mass murder took place and, second, that the victims were not soldiers fighting in a battle.

Many witnesses would testify in court to the genocide. But were their stories backed up by physical evidence – by proof written in the bones?

That was the key question for the PHR team. Clea helped dig up two mass graves in Rwanda, patch by patch and layer by layer. After carefully digging up a section, she marked the location of each corpse with a red flag and counted the skulls, one per body. Deeper in the grave, she would find 'fleshed bodies' – whole corpses. But in the tropical warmth, many bodies near the surface were already skeletons or natural mummies.

The first step was to map the Kibuye church grounds, a complex of 22 buildings, and search for skeletons on the surface.

The forensic team dug layer by careful layer into the mass grave. Each body was photographed in place and then moved to the autopsy tent.

The forensic team separate and examine the jumble of bones found in a grave.

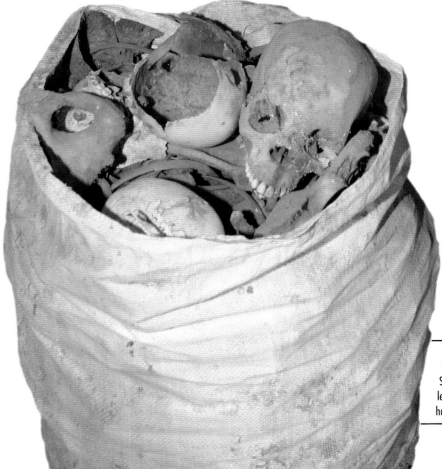

A 13-year-old survivor named Valentina Iribagiza hid among dead bodies, badly wounded. She said, "I did not think that anybody was left alive in the country. I thought everybody had been swept away."

35

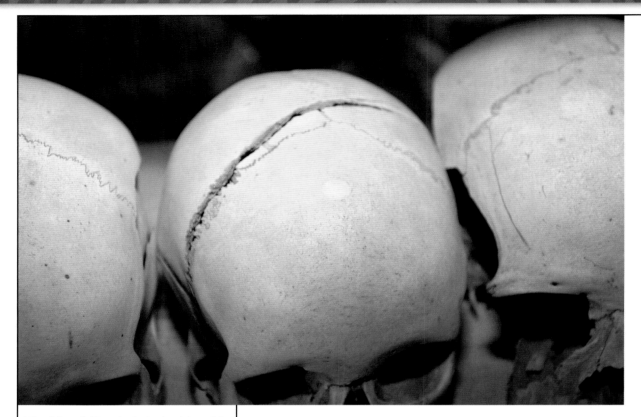

A Hutu killer called Tutsis 'snakes' and said that to kill snakes, 'you must smash their heads'. Skull after skull showed evidence of bone crushing, fatal blows.

After uncovering the remains, Clea sorted the bones into individual skeletons. She paired right arms with left arms, for example, using an observation technique called 'siding'. She placed the bone sets in anatomical order – where they belong on a body – on separate autopsy tables. They were photographed as a set, and then in close-up, especially the wounds.

The cause of death was easy to read, even for a non-expert. Clea noted all the breaks, cuts, cracks, and holes on the skulls and other bones. Time after time, she wrote down 'sharp force trauma' and 'blunt force trauma' in her reports. Witnesses had said the killers used broad, sharp blades called machetes and clubs.

The bones said so, too. Many wounds were to the back of the head and body. The victims were attacked from behind. Clea checked for defence wounds – injuries to hands and arms raised to protect the head or chest. She found none. The victims hadn't – or couldn't – fight back. Clearly, they weren't soldiers in a battle. The manner of death, Clea wrote over and over again, was 'murder'.

Clea couldn't put names to the skeletons, but she used all her anthropology skills to identify their sex, age, height, and ancestry. Were these people mostly men or women? Children or adults? Like the wounds, this data would provide shocking proof of genocide.

36

Sizing up skeletons

Adult male skeletons are generally larger and sturdier than female skeletons. Men have bigger muscles, on the whole, and so need bigger bones to carry them. But have you ever met a man who was skinny and on the small side, or a woman who was big and strong? Size alone is a poor clue for identifying male and female bones. To determine sex, Clea looked first at the shape of the pelvic girdle (the hip bones) and then at certain features of the skull.

The pelvic bones show clear differences because women have children and men don't. Skulls have finer variations – like the sharp edges of the eye sockets of a woman and the brow ridges that tend to stick out on a man. A female chin is often slender and pointy; a man's chin is likely to be squared off.

If you look closely at lots of faces, you'll find that these guidelines aren't foolproof. You can easily find a man with a pointy chin and a woman with a big brow ridge. That's why Clea looked at lots of features before deciding 'male' or 'female' – or any identifier.

She estimated the age of children based on the growth of teeth and bones, which change quickly and dramatically from birth to adulthood. Many of the victims were under the age of five – infants and toddlers.

About one in four bodies were under 10.

In adults, age is trickier. All the teeth are in place, and the bones have grown. Wear and tear is a general clue – older bones and teeth tend to show more signs of disease and break-down. But a best estimate for adult age might be as wide as 30s to early 50s.

To determine a height range, Clea measured femurs (thigh bones) or other long bones. If you stand next to someone taller than you and someone shorter, who has the longest thigh, from knee cap to the bottom of the hip? Chances are, it's the tallest person, but it's not always easy to tell.

More than 5,000 Tutsis flocked to Ntarama church near Kigali, the capital of Rwanda, thinking they would be safe. Instead, they became trapped inside. Hutu extremists killed all but a handful.

After the slaughter, Tutsis turned the Ntarama church into a memorial. Bloody clothes, bones, and broken skulls, tell a story of horror to anyone with the courage to visit.

37

MASS GRAVE AT THE KIBUYE ROMAN CATHOLIC CHURCH

- **Location:** Kibuye, Rwanda
- **Bodies examined:** 493
- **Identifications by name:** 17 (identified by ID cards, clothing, and personal items)
- **Women and children:** 74% of victims
- **Children under 10:** 25% of victims
- **Manner of death:** Murder
- **Cause of death:** Sharp force and blunt force trauma (cuts from machetes and blows from clubs)

To make very precise measurements, Clea used an an osteometric ('bone measure') board. It looks like a foot measuring tool at a shoe store – only more exact. She entered the bone length into an equation based on measuring thousands of bones of people of known height. The equation gives a range of probable heights, like 152 cm to 165 cm, that apply to 95 percent of people. The other 5 percent have an unusually long femur for a short body or an unusually short femur for a tall body.

Justice, families, and the future

Using these methods and others, Clea and the PHR team came up with a shocking number: 70 percent of the Kibuye victims – seven out of 10 – were women and children. Their data from Kibuye and Kigali, the other Rwanda site, helped prove the case of genocide against many powerful people, including a prime minister, a governor, and other leaders. As of July 2006, the world court has convicted 25 people in trials expected to last four more years.

Forensic anthropologists have dug up similar mass graves in countries like Argentina, Guatemala, Iraq, Afghanistan, and others. Their goals are to help bring killers to justice and to let families know what happened to missing loved ones.

Clea explains, "You realise that you're the first person to see the bodies since the killers buried them, thinking they got away with the crime. That's when you are motivated to keep uncovering the truth. It's not just for the victims, but for their families too."

Groups like the PHR have a bigger goal, too. They hope to spread the word about genocides and mass murders of the past to prevent more deaths in the future.

A few survivors recognised loved ones by the jewellery or personal items found on the body. Clea Koff was moved by a pretty pink necklace that stood out in the mass grave at Kibuye.

ON THE CASE:

GROUND ZERO
AFTER 9/11

After two jumbo jets smashed into the twin towers of the World Trade Center in New York City, there was no need to determine manner and cause of death. The date, 11 September, 2001, is etched in history as the worst terrorist attack ever.

The date, 11 September, 2001, is etched in history as the worst terrorist attack ever – murder on a massive scale.

Both giant towers fell to pieces in clouds of dust, killing 2,749 people. Two other jets, also taken by terrorists, crashed that day; one hit the Pentagon in Washington, D.C., and another crashed into the ground in Pennsylvania.

Dozens of forensic pathologists, pathologists, forensic anthropologists, and other doctors and scientists of the dead were called to New York for one reason: to help identify the victims. The experts were organised by a government group called DMORT (Disaster Mortuary Operational Response Team).

All the volunteers worked long hours, sifting through the rubble and bits of debris, looking for human remains. They bagged and tagged everything they found. The evidence filled 18 large, refrigerated trucks.

Personal items, fingerprints, medical records, dental records, and other means – all means available, in fact – were used to identify the remains at the site. DNA tests alone have named about 850 people – one-third of the total.

In April 2005, the New York city M.E.'s (medical examiner) office declared any further identification impossible, leaving nearly two-thirds of the remains forever unknown.

For months after the 11 September attack, World Trade Center debris was shipped across the harbour to Staten Island. Anthropologists and forensic pathologists helped spot human remains while investigators looked for personal items to identify victims.

Anyone can give an opinion about anything. But an expert opinion is more than an idea or a belief. It's a conclusion – a reasonable explanation – based on evidence and on the medical knowledge of the examiner. In an autopsy report, a forensic pathologist lists the autopsy findings in detail and explains what that evidence means.

Facts are facts, but experts may still interpret those facts differently. Experts can, and often do, disagree about what the evidence means.

In 1997, the fate of a 19-year-old British nanny hinged on expert opinions that were all over the medical map.

Murder or accident?

On 4 February, 1997, Louise Woodward was taking care of baby Matthew for the Eappen family of Massachusetts, US. The eight-month-old had been crying all day. But now, he wasn't breathing well, and his skin was blue. The nanny called for an ambulance.

Though no injuries could be seen outside of the body, x-rays revealed a skull fracture.

Dr. Joseph Madsen operated on the brain, but Matthew died a few days later.

An autopsy report listed the cause of death as blunt force trauma to the head – no doubt there. But was the manner of death murder or accident? How did the fracture happen? Was it a new injury from the day of the nanny's emergency call? Or did it occur weeks earlier, under someone else's care?

These questions had no easy answers. Louise Woodward went on trial for murder, a trial that featured 15 medical experts!

Dr. Madsen said the head injury was new and not accidental. He blamed, "A severe blow to the head against a blunt surface and additional swinging or shaking of the head." He believed there were signs of Shaken Baby Syndrome (SBS) – the baby had been picked up and violently shaken. One sign was bleeding at the back of the eyes. This was confirmed by Dr. Lois Smith, an eye expert.

An x-ray expert agreed the head injuries were 'suggestive of' SBS and looked new. A new fracture has sharp edges that haven't started to heal. Yet another x-ray expert said that the

Dr. Jan Leestma, a forensic pathologist who specialises in the nervous system, told the court that Matthew Eappen's brain began bleeding three weeks before the 8-month-old baby died. Was the trauma injury an accident or murder? Impossible to tell, said the doctor.

same fracture was three or four weeks old. An old fracture has rounded edges with a lip. Which was it – sharp or rounded?

Dr. Jan Leestma, a forensic pathologist, said the head injury was about three weeks old based on the colour of blood in the brain. Fresh blood is bright red. Old blood is blackish-red, brownish, or yellowish. He also said the eye bleeding was due to pressure from the head injury – not from shaking.

Dr. Gerald Feigin had performed the autopsy, with help from three brain experts. He didn't agree with SBS, but he insisted the fracture happened on 4 February, the day of the emergency call. One brain expert put the date as "no earlier than" 2 February.

You can see the challenge. The medical experts testified for days, going over the same evidence, agreeing and disagreeing. The jury found Louise Woodward guilty of murder, but a judge later lowered the charge to manslaughter.

What if, some day, you're on a jury and have to sort out expert opinions like these? Your decision could mean freedom or prison for another human being.

On pages 42 and 43, you will read part of a real autopsy report, though the victim's name is withheld for privacy.

What's your opinion?

Guilty of second degree murder! This shocking verdict meant the jury believed Louise Woodward killed baby Matthew with 'malice' – out of meanness, hatred, or cruelty.

Judge Hiller Zobel lowered the murder conviction to 'involuntary manslaughter'. He said Louise Woodward acted out of 'confusion, inexperience, frustration, immaturity, and some anger but not malice'. The British nanny was freed after spending 279 days (almost 10 months) in jail.

ON THE CASE:

THE CALIFORNIA JOGGER

On 14 February, 2000, a crime scene investigator in San Diego, California, reported:

At 4:36 p.m., a deputy found the body of a man, age 55, near a remote mountain road. The man's wife had reported him missing the evening before. She had last seen him, dressed in jogging clothes, at about 1 p.m. (the day before) at their ranch home. She said the man often ran along the road where his body was found. The body was "cold to the touch and in full rigor mortis."

The next day, a forensic pathologist performed an autopsy and then wrote a 15-page report.

- What evidence did the doctor find?
- What expert opinions did he form?

There's a hidden twist to this case!

Read the key parts of the autopsy evidence, then think like a crime scientist about what that evidence means:

- What was the manner of death?
- What was the cause of death?

- What is the estimated time of death?
- Was the body moved or altered after death?
- What can you infer about the murder weapon based on the injuries?

On pages 44 and 45 you can read the forensic pathologist's surprising conclusion.

THE AUTOPSY REPORT

Office of the San Diego County

Forensic Pathologist

Autopsy Report: Case 00-0335

Date of autopsy: 15 February, 2000

Time of autopsy: 9:45 a.m. to 2:45 p.m.

CLOTHING AND INITIAL OBSERVATIONS

- All the clothing was removed at the scene (by investigators) except for the blue boxers.
- Around the upper waistband (of the boxers) is dark red staining.
- The rope that was around the neck is a braided black cloth rope approximately 111 cm in length and is 0.79 cm in diameter. One end is frayed. The rope is bloody and damp.
- A sheet is around the body and bags are on the head, hands and feet.
- There is blood staining around the right side of the head, neck, and upper torso. Some blood is also seen on the arms.
- There is blood on the [palm] of the left hand… and the right hand.
- Overlying the upper torso (but under the man's clothing) when initially viewed at the scene is a small, triangular piece of scalp which measures 1.27 cm and has attached brown and gray hair measuring slightly greater than 5 cm in length.

- There is a small amount of dirt and scattered leaves on the back (of the body).

EXTERNAL DESCRIPTION

- Rigor mortis is still moderately well developed, although it has been partially broken in the arms.
- Lividity is posterior (on the back) and sparse; on the anterior (front) upper torso and shoulders. More lividity is noted on the [middle] of the right arm throughout most of its extent.
- The head hair is brown with… gray measuring 6-7 cm in length.
- There are fine petechiae (on the eyeball) and the right upper lateral eyelid.

EXTERNAL EVIDENCE OF INJURIES

The report lists eight head injuries, labelled A to H. Injuries A and B are different deep cuts:

A) A 5.7 cm laceration. This is slightly curved with a central width of approximately 0.95 cm. There are a few tiny lacerations at the edges. The laceration extends down to the bone where there is a depressed (dented) skull fracturing.

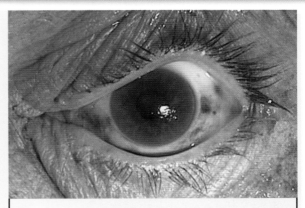

Those red spots on the eyeball form when capillaries burst and leak blood. Pinpoint blood specks are called petechiae; larger ones are called purpura.

B) On the back of the head is a large, jagged, irregular laceration measuring 8.8 x 4.4 cm. It extends down to the underlying bone so that the brain matter is exposed.

- fine petechiae (on the eyeball)
- On the neck is a horizontal, superficial (surface-only) red-purple ligature mark 0.95 cm in width.

INTERNAL EXAMINATION

This section describes the badly injured head, body cavity, organs, and body systems.

- Neck: there is a fracture through the left horn of the hyoid bone. The hyoid bone is intact with fused joints.
- Gastrointestinal system: the stomach contains approximately 450 ml of mixed food including red meat, light green leafy vegetable, white potato, beans and small fragments of red pepper (or tomato).

Now turn to the next page to read the conclusion to the case. . .

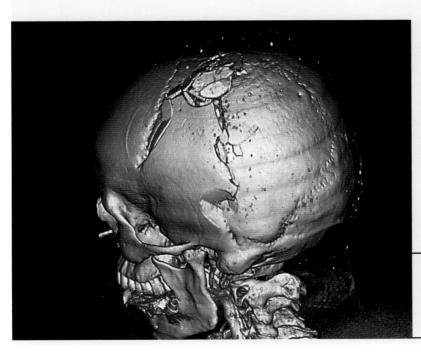

This 40-year-old man survived several hard, high-speed blows to the head. A CT scan (three-dimensional x-ray) reveals depressed fractures, places where skull bone was pushed in toward the brain.

ON THE CASE:

THE CALIFORNIA JOGGER

A SURPRISING CONCLUSION
CONTINUED…

Was a 55-year-old California man killed while out running? That's what his wife suggested to police. She told them he was dressed to go jogging at about 1 p.m. the day before his body was found (which would have been 13 February). Was she telling the truth?

MANNER/CAUSE

The M.E. ruled the manner of death a murder. Blood, a rope around the neck, and head injuries made that fact clear.

And the cause of death? He concluded it was 'blunt force head injuries'. The deadliest blows were to the back and right side of the head.

The murder weapon was never found, but a tool mark expert said head injury A was consistent with the round head of a hammer, and head injury B matched the two-pronged claw end.

The M.E. listed 'ligature strangulation' as a 'contributing factor'. The rope left a mark on the neck, and a broken hyoid bone and petechiae are common in strangulation cases. The M.E. couldn't tell if the strangling, "Occurred before, after, or during the head injuries."

Stomach contents last about 2 to 4 hours. The corpse was cold and in full rigor mortis at 4:36 p.m., the time it was found. Death happened hours, not minutes and not days earlier. The wife claimed her husband was alive at 1 p.m. the day before. Yet the autopsy report says the body still had a lot of rigor two days later. As you read earlier in the book, rigor can vary due to temperature, moisture, and other factors.

So, did the man die shortly after he left the house? Or later in the evening?

The autopsy report doesn't say. The range of possible times is too broad to be useful.

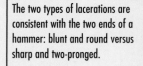

The two types of lacerations are consistent with the two ends of a hammer: blunt and round versus sharp and two-pronged.

TIME SINCE DEATH?

Saying "when" is always tricky. The undigested food in the stomach means the man ate before he died. But was it lunch or dinner? An autopsy can't determine that. It can only suggest about how long before death he had his last meal.

WHERE'S THE CRIME SCENE?

Was the man killed where he was found, or killed elsewhere and dumped along that road? The M.E. listed the location of the crime as 'undetermined', but there's a 'smoking gun'-type clue in the autopsy report. Did you spot it?

A THEORY

Beneath the man's jogging clothes, on his chest, was a tiny piece of scalp. The hairs matched his hair colour and length. Detectives concluded that the man was beaten first, and then dressed in fresh jogging clothes!

So what about the wife's story? The autopsy report and other clues led detectives back to the victim's ranch. As they searched a seemingly spotless house, they soon discovered why it appeared so squeaky clean. In the bedroom, they found tiny blood spatters on the walls and ceiling. They lifted the carpet and found that a pool of blood had seeped through the floor into the room below.

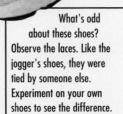

What's odd about these shoes? Observe the laces. Like the jogger's shoes, they were tied by someone else. Experiment on your own shoes to see the difference.

Piecing together the clues, the detectives came up with a theory: the wife beat and strangled her husband in the bedroom. She dressed his body in fresh clothes and dumped it along his favourite jogging path.

She tried hard to clean up the crime scene and then reported her husband 'missing'. In 2001, a California jury convicted the wife of murder. She is serving 25 years to life in prison.

Case 00-0335

CASE CLOSED

Glossary

algor mortis ('cold death'): The gradual change in body temperature of a fresh corpse to match the air temperature.

autopsy: A medical examination, inside and out, of a corpse to determine the manner and cause of death. The word comes from the Greek *autós* ('self') and *op* ('see') – 'see for yourself'.

cause of death: The medical reason a person died – blunt force trauma, drowning, gunshot wound, and so on.

coroner: A person elected to take charge of death cases in an American county. No medical training is needed.

DNA: A molecule present in every life form and contains sequences of chemicals that form the 'code of life' – the genetic instructions for making a plant, animal, or other organism. The letters stand for DeoxyriboNucleic Acid.

forensic: Describes anything or anyone having to do with evidence in a crime case or accident, such as a plane crash.

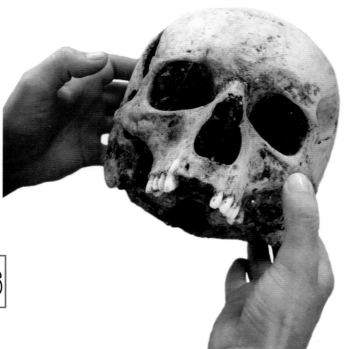

forensic pathologist: A doctor (called a Medical Examiner or M.E. in the US) who performs autopsies and is trained in interpreting injuries as evidence to determine manner and cause of death.

genocide: The attempt to kill off a large group of people who share a race, religion, or other cultural trait. The Greek root '*genus*' means 'race' or 'kind'.

haemorrhage: Bleeding, which can be internal (inside the body) or external (outside).

homicide: One person killing another. Murder is the most serious form of homicide. From the Latin *homo* ('man') and *cide* ('kill'). Homicide can also be assisted suicide (helping someone die on purpose) or manslaughter (a less serious charge than murder).

ligature: Any type of cord used to tie or strangle someone. Ligatures often leave a ligature mark – a telltale bruise.

livor mortis ('blue death'): Also called lividity, it's the post-death pooling of blood in low spots, due to gravity.

manner of death: One of five categories, including natural, accident, suicide, murder, or undetermined.

petechiae: Tiny, dark blood specks caused by burst capillaries. They are a sign of possible strangulation or suffocation.

rigor mortis ('rigid death'): The gradual and temporary stiffening of the muscles shortly after death.

trauma: Damage to the body from blunt force (like a blow), sharp force (like a cut), or a projectile (like a bullet

BOOKS

The Body Book, by Sara Stein (Workman, 1992). If you're thinking of becoming a forensic pathologist, here's a good start for 'boning up' on body system basics.

Bone Detective: The Story of Forensic Anthropologist Diane France, by Lorraine Jean Hopping (Joseph Henry Press, 2006). The life story of a small-town girl who fell in love with bones and became a bone detective in order to speak for the dead in cases of murder and mass accident.

Silent Witness: How Forensic Anthropology is Used to Solve the World's Toughest Crimes, by Roxana Ferllini. Rich in colour photos, you can see for yourself how bone detectives interpret evidence.

WEB SITES

Andes Expedition: Searching for Inca Secrets: National Geographic's online site about a mummified Incan princess includes a virtual autopsy of the body through CT scan images.
http://www.nationalgeographic.com/features/97/andes/

Forensic Entomology: Cases studies in which insects made good clocks to establish time of death and other facts.
http://www.forensic-entomology.com/

HBO's Interactive Autopsy: Using a model, Dr. Michael Baden steps you through the whole autopsy operation, outside and in.
http://www.hbo.com/autopsy/interactive/index.html

Human Anatomy Online: This interactive, illustrated guide to 10 body systems (skeletal, digestive, muscular, nervous, and so on) is helpful as a general reference and research tool. There are a few simple animations that show how things work.
http://www.innerbody.com/index.html

The Virtual Autopsy Game: Read a case file, 'examine' the interactive body (including real autopsy photos and medical notes), and see if you can pick out the cause of death from a list.
http://www.le.ac.uk/pa/teach/va/titlpag1.html

The Virtual Body: Tour the brain, skeleton, heart, and digestive tract (in English or Spanish), play anatomy games, and research biology facts using interactive body part maps.
http://www.medtropolis.com/VBody.asp

The Bone Woman: The website of Clea Koff, who wrote a book about her experiences investigating mass graves around the world.
http://www.thebonewoman.com/

International Centre of Excellence for the Investigation of Genocide: News and information about mass graves and the trials of those who created them.
http://inforce.org.uk/index.htm

American Board of Forensic Entomology: How to use the life cycles of bugs to determine the time and sometimes the location of death, including case studies.
http://www.research.missouri.edu/entomology/

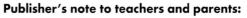

Publisher's note to teachers and parents:
Our editors have carefully reviewed these Web sites to ensure that they are suitable for children. Many Web sites change frequently, however, and we cannot guarantee that a site's future contents will continue to meet our high standards of quality and educational value. Be advised that children should be closely supervised whenever they access the Internet.

Index